THE
APOTHECARY

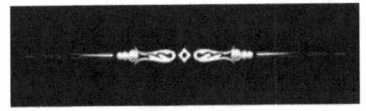

Green Cheesecake at Midnight

Book 1

THE
APOTHECARY

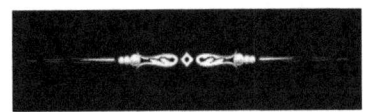

Green Cheesecake at Midnight

copyright © 2010 by T.S. Cherry

All rights reserved. No part of this publication may be reproduced, distributed, or transmitted in any form or by any means, including photocopying, recording, or other electronic or mechanical methods, without the prior written permission of the publisher, except in the case of brief quotations embodied in critical reviews and certain other noncommercial uses permitted by copyright law. For permission requests, write to the publisher, addressed "Attention: Permissions Coordinator," at the address below.

Tiil Books
www.tiil.org.com

Ordering Information:
Quantity sales. Special discounts are available on quantity purchases by corporations, associations, and others. For details, contact the publisher at the address above.
Orders by U.S. trade bookstores and wholesalers

visit www.tiil.org

Printed in the United States of America

Tiil.org

by

T.S. Cherry

Tiil Books

The church is dark. Candles have been lit, white and silver; these melting towers of wax, Katie has never hated them more before than she does right now. Religion has never been a main part of her family. They go to church on Sunday because, that's habit - tradition, almost. They say grace at Thanksgiving. They smile at people as they pass, because that's just how things go.

It's never been something that Katie felt completely comfortable with. The idea of an all seeing God - it makes her skin crawl!

To think there's someone watching her all the time? Katie shudders at the mere thought.

Right now, though, it feels like no one is watching her.

Katie sits in the front row of the pews. Her hands are folded in her lap, fingers clasp each other in a white knuckled grip. Everyone is silent.

The preacher talks, but his voice is a low sort of drone. The very air seems heavy with exhaustion, desperation, and a grief that can't ever be erased.

This is why: Isabella Rite is dead.

And Katie Rite, she doesn't think that it's something she'll ever get past. Her mother has always been an integral part of her life. They were as close as any mother and daughter could be; for the bond between mother and child is unavoidable, and it's undeniable, and it is unexplainable.

Right now, the only unexplainable thing for Katie is why it feels like she's so utterly alone. There are other people here; family friends, cousins, and even a few strangers that she swears have never shown face in the Rite household.

No one will look at her.

No one will talk to her.

Katie's chest is tight. It's suddenly hard to breathe. The church is oppressive. It's draining her. It's ruining her.

She stands up. No one looks her way. Katie doesn't realize she's crying until her cheeks are wet, until it's hard to pull in a proper breath of air. "I have to get out of here," she gasps. "I have to get out of here!"

Katie spins around on her heels. She storms out of the church; like the building is the source of all her sorrows, all her rage.

It's not, of course, because the church had nothing to do with Isabella's death. Still, it feels good to have something to blame. When Katie bursts out of the church, she feels like she can breathe again. The city air is clear, is light. The sun feels good on her skin.

The doors close with a low thud.

As Katie rounds the corner, she hears the doors close a second time. The sound, for a reason that Katie can't quite explain, makes her heart skip a beat. She takes off, running down the sidewalk, racing down the street with nowhere to go, with no goal but *leave, go, move.*

It sounds like someone is running after her. When Katie looks over her shoulder, she only sees empty streets. The city is a small enough thing. Most of the streets are lined with local businesses, the sort that everyone loves, the sort that everyone visits. And yet, there are shadows on the streets; there are alleys that need to be explored and buildings that have been built, only to be abandoned later when the funding runs out.

It's strange, this town. Katie loves it. The mix of old and new - of dead and living. But, right then, right now, she still feels like it's crushing her. Worse, she feels like there's something following her, hiding in the shadows, in the wayward bursts of pale yellow street lights and alley way entrances.

Looking behind her proves nothing. While the city isn't empty, Katie is certainly not alone. No one had been watching her in the church…but someone is watching her now.

The only solution, as far as Katie can tell, is to go somewhere safe.

For her, it used to be home. But now, with her mother dead and gone, home doesn't feel that protected. It's as though the locks no longer work, as though the brick walls that were once so cozy have now turned into impenetrable blocks; they don't keep Katie safe, they merely keep her pinned down.

And so, she heads for Denny Lowe's house instead.

Katie and Denny have been friends since forever. The two girls grew up with each other, and have done virtually everything together – first haircut, first day of school, first lost tooth – first failing grade, first time sneaking out, and even the first kiss, this messy thing traded in the dark of the Lowe's spare bedroom, because Denny wanted to try kissing her boyfriend but didn't want to make a fool of herself.

If there's any safe place left in this city, it's at the Lowe's house.

Now, one would think that, since Denny and Katie are such good friends, the Lowe's would have been invited to Isabella's funeral. Unfortunately, Isabella and Mathew Lowe, Denny's father, had never gotten along. As such, they refused to come, and Katie's father refused to invite them.

Katie hadn't seen it as an upside until right now. She lets herself into the Lowe's house, using the key that she's had since forever.

"It's just me," she shouts.

From the kitchen, Mathew says, "It's good to see you, Katie. Denny's upstairs, studying. You want a sandwich?"

"No thank you!" Katie shouts out.

"Are you sure? I'm making fried bologna and cheese!" Mathew shouts back.

"I'm really not hungry," insists Katie, toeing off her shoes and making one last look behind her before she closes the door. "But thank you, Mr Lowe!"

"Alright," says Mathew. "You just let me know if you change your mind. I've got plenty, and it's just going in the fridge for now."

"I will," promises Katie. Following the rules of the Lowe house hold, she pulls off her socks and tucks them neatly into her worn red sneakers before taking off up the stairs. She takes the steps two at a time.

The hallway of the top floor is brightly lit, with family pictures hanging on the walls and a different color paint slathered on every door. Denny's room is marked with dark orange paint and a single white circle right at the center.

It's supposed to mean good luck, but Katie isn't sure how. Denny only ever shrugs when the question is brought up.

Katie knocks once, but opens up the door without waiting to be called. "It's just me," she says quickly, trying to stop Denny's frantic scramble to hide her *batman* comic book behind the pages of her science textbook.

The two girls look nothing alike. Katie is tall and scrawny, with naturally dark skin and kinky black hair. Her eyes are wide set, her nails always bitten short, and her clothing a pleasant mix of lace and black skulls. On the other end of the spectrum, Denny is short and plump, with a love for vintage clothing and rainbow dyed hair shaved to the scalp on one half of her head, pulled into a braid on the other.

She lets out a relieved sigh when she realizes that it's just Katie. "Thank God," breathes Denny. "I thought you were my mom, for sure."

"No," says Katie, with a nervous laugh. "It's just me! Hey, can I - are you busy?"

Denny rolls onto her side, patting the bed in welcome. "Am I ever?"

"Not really. I just - this is kind of important." Katie sits down by Denny's feet, which have blue and green alternating painted nails.

Denny pushes herself up, swinging her legs over the edge of the bed saying, "Is it about your mom?"

"No. Well, yes. Sort of?" Katie responds.

"I'm all ears, Katie Cat. You know that," Denny says smiling.

"I know. I just - this is going to sound really weird. I was at her memorial - that was today, you know," Katie says in a strained tone.

Denny nods, patiently. She has star plugs in the lobes of her stretched out ears. "I know. I'm not going to say *I'm sorry* though, because I bet you're sick of that."

"Like crazy," admits Katie, sheepishly. "But that's actually not the problem. I just - I couldn't stand being in there any longer, you know? I couldn't stand being in there any longer, so I took off outside... and I think someone followed me!"

Denny doesn't laugh, but she doesn't look overly concerned either. "They were probably concerned about you."

"No, it wasn't that. Every time I looked over my shoulder, whoever it was must have been hiding. But I could hear them following me," Katie explains. "The door closing after I left, the sound of their footsteps. This sounds silly, because I didn't see her, and I don't have any proof, but I think it might have been Miss Green."

"What makes you say that?" Denny asks.

"She's been acting weird all day. And I mean, weirder than usual," says Katie.

Denny nods, "Is it worth pointing out that she and your mom were super close?"

Katie shakes her head, "That's not it. It's more than that. She's been weird in a creepy way. She keeps staring at my dad."

"Is she into him?" Denny cocks her eyebrow.

"Ugh, no way! She's like twenty years older!" Katie wrinkles her nose, disgusted at the idea.

"That doesn't mean she can't be into him," says Denny, idly. "But if you're really worked up about it, we could just check it out ourselves."

"How?" Katie asks

"By going to her store, duh!" Denny rolls her eyes. "Miss Green has all kinds of weird things in that shop."

Katie says, "All Apothecary stores are weird."

"That's true," agrees Denny, nodding. "But you can't tell me you've ever been in one more weird than Miss Green's."

"I've never been in one that was *as* weird as Miss Green's," admits Katie.

"Then there we go," says Denny, even though nothing has really been decided. "We'll case her store this weekend."

"Case it?" questions Katie.

"To see what weird brews she has cooking," Denny explains. "You know, Cassie is pretty sure that she's a witch."

"There's no such thing as witches!" scoffs Katie.

"There might be," says Denny, firmly. "There might be witches out here. You never know. And if there's going to be a witch, I'm positive that it's Miss Green. She's batty."

"Wouldn't that make her a vampire?" Katie cracks a small smile. It's easy to joke with Denny, even though the whole world seems kind of horrible right now.

Denny lets out a bellowing laugh, "Okay, then she's a vampire witch! Problem solved! There's your answer about why she's been so weird."

"Not the answer I was looking for," laughs Katie, but she drops backwards onto the bed. The mattress is new. It doesn't so much as creak once. "But it's pretty close, I guess."

Denny drops backwards, too. She throws out her arms to the side so their fingers are touching. "We'll figure this out, Katie. If there's something going on, you know we'll find out what."

As much as Katie would like to just spend eternity at the Lowe's house, that's not actually an option. The young girl does, eventually, have to push herself up and go home. It's not a welcome feeling. The house is just as oppressive as the church. It sucks the life out of her, stepping through those front doors.

Katie pushes her shoes off but leaves her socks on. The lights are turned down low. Blankets have been hung up in front of the mirrors, and heavy drapes have been pulled shut before the windows.

Her father is in the living room, watching home movies. He's still in his black suit.

Katie smooths out the front of her dress, suddenly feeling self-conscious. She clears her throat and walks into the living room. She says, "Dad, can I talk to you?"

He sniffs, loudly, "I didn't remember this part."

"What?" Katie says taken off-guard.

"In the video," he dad says. "I didn't remember how happy your mother looked."

Katie sits down on the couch next to her father, "I know. I miss her too."

"She looks so happy," sniffs Sam. "Do you remember the last time she looked like this?"

"Before she got sick," says Katie, without hesitation. "She looked like this right before she got sick."

"I don't know why it happened to her," laments Sam.

Katie asks, "What do you know about her friendship with Miss Green?"

"That poor woman," says Sam. "We're going to need to make sure we stop by and visit her, now that your mother isn't h— isn't able too."

"Were they really good friends?" Katie asks.

"The best," Sam says with a sigh.

"Did she tell you what they did every Saturday?" Katie continues to question.

Sam points at the television, "Look at this, Katie. Watch your mother here."

Katie sighs, but pats her pet dog oodles and looks at the television. She got even less out of her father today then she did yesterday, and twice as little as the day before. It seems, with each passing moment, that the man is drifting farther away from her.

He doesn't want to talk. He just wants to sit here and dream about a better time.

Saturday comes with a flurry of rain and heavy gray clouds that hang low in the sky. Katie pulls on her rain slick and her rubber boots. She grabs her purse, pausing at the door just long enough to shout, "Good bye, dad!"

There's no answer. Recorded laughter booms out of the television speakers. Katie has never hated those videos more in her life. She slams the door behind herself and takes off down the street.

Miss Green's Apothecary Store for the Fearless and Bold, as it's called, is located out near the square. Katie meets up with her friends in a nearby coffee shop. They all order a round of pumpkin spice low fat almond milk lattes, topped with extra whipped cream.

Katie lingers at the counter, "Can I get an extra shot of espresso in mine?"

"Sure," sighs the cashier.

Denny stares at Katie like she's just grown three heads, "You're adding something?"

"Yes?" Katie sighs with sarcasm.

"But we all decided ages ago that the lattes were perfect *just* like this!" Denny squawks.

"I'm not sleeping well"' admits Katie. "I keep dreaming about my mother."

No one questions her latte choices after that. The girls all gather around a table once their drinks are served. Along with Denny, a boy named Carl and a younger girl named Tabby have shown up.

Tabby asks, "So, what's the plan?"

"There is no plan," says Carl, in that nasal voice of his. "Those two never have a plan!"

Denny huffs, "We do too have a plan!"

Carl demands, "Yeah? So what is it?"

"We're going to Miss Green's. You and Tabby are going to ask a bunch of questions about some of her more weird wares," says Denny, firmly. "I'm going to serve as watch and blocker. If you lose her, I'll cause a distraction and get her back in the main room. Katie here is going to try and find something that might prove she's a witch."

Katie snorts, "I'm going to try and find out why she was following me."

"And if she's a witch," says Denny, again. "That's a really important part of this whole thing."

"Is it really?" Katie shrugs.

"Yes! It's probably the most important part!" Denny scolds. "If she's a witch, then there doesn't need to be a reason for why she's following you. It will obviously have to do with one of her witchy ceremonies!"

Katie rolls her eyes, "Right. The point is, I'm going to see what I can find out."

"Okay," says Tabby, shrugging her shoulders. "It's not like I've got anything better to do right now."

And so the group of teenagers finish their absurdly detailed pumpkin spice lattes, pay their bills, and vanish back into the cold and dreary day.

"This place gives me the creeps," mutters Tabby, stepping up to the front door of Miss Green's shop. It doesn't look like most of the other stores in the square, with cracked windows, a chipped up front door, and all manner of spiders and bugs in the front walk way.

A cloud of dust, muss, and other unfortunate things comes rushing into their faces. The shop is old and seldom visited. It's filled with strange curiosities, the likes of which no normal person would find of interest. Antique marble statues are wedged into the corner, with dream catchers and bundles of dried herbs, and bottles full of tinctures and potions all with *for sale* hanging off of them. Golden covered picture frames cling to the walls, filled with oil portraits straight from a horror movie.

An old bell chimes when the door opens. Miss Green is nowhere to be seen. Still, the group of friends put their plan into action!

Tabby and Carl start poking around on the shelves filled with the various knick-knacks, small clay bowls, and hand carved idols. They talk, loudly, bickering about the prices and the possible uses for the objects.

"I don't think so," says Tabby, loud on purpose. "There's no way that's from China. Look at it! It's clearly Korean!"

Carl snorts. He tosses the small green turtle from one palm to the next. It's made from some sort of marble. "That's just stupid. It's obviously Chinese. Look at the markings on the back of the shell. That's obviously kanji made to look like shell blocks."

The argument is pointless. Neither teenager has any clue where the turtle came from, nor do they care.

Slowly, Katie creeps into the back room. She can see Miss Green's tall spindly form bent over a recently acquired crate of wares, sorting the objects into different piles. She waves Denny in and ducks behind a large metal shelf. It's filled up with an odd assortment of glass baubles.

Denny flounces over to Miss Green. She taps the old woman on the shoulder, "Miss Green? I was hoping to ask you a few questions."

The old woman sighs; her breath reeks of peppermint, "Yes, Denny?"

Denny blinks, "How do you know my name?"

"I just do," says Miss Green. "Now, what did you want to ask me about? Please tell me it's not the turtle that your friend is talking about."

"No! Wait - how do you know about that?" Denny asks, shocked that Miss Green heard her friends but made no move to stop them from touching the items.

"It's my store," answers Miss Green. "Why wouldn't I know about it?"

Denny gives Katie a concerned glance. She says, "I don't know. It just seemed strange."

"Your pointless questions seem strange," counters Miss Green. "I was hoping you had an actual question. I'm a busy woman."

Katie waves at Denny from behind the shelf system.

Denny says, "no! I do have a question! You have a - uh - a wooden thing out there. It's super neat looking, but I haven't got a clue what it is. Could you tell me?"

Miss Green sighs. She wipes her hands off on her skirt. "Yes, alright. Show me what you're looking at."

Katie waits until Denny and Miss Green have vanished from the back room before she starts looking around. Now, snooping is hard to do even when you know what you're looking for, but it's even more difficult when you've got no clue about what's happening. In the end, the only item that catches Katie's eye is a bottle of *Wash Away the Blues* shampoo.

For some reason, Katie can't shake the feeling that it's important. She slips the bottle inside her rain slicker and makes her way back into the main room of the shop just before Miss Green goes back into the back room.

Denny says, "You ow me big time," and then hooks an arm around Katie's waist, hauling her outside.

What no one thinks about, though, is that Miss Green is a very old woman. She's an old woman that lives alone, works alone, and generally spends most of her time alone. That means she's gotten smart over the years.

The security camera's pinned up all over the shelf run to a video system and a television in the small side office, which is hidden from view by a massive golden, purple, and red quilt that hangs from the ceiling.

As soon as the group of teenagers leave, Miss Green steps into her office. It smells like cinnamon. She sits down in a bear claw chair and pulls up the recording of the last fifteen minutes.

It's plain as day that Katie has just stolen from her, and even more plain is what's been pocketed.

"That fool," says Miss Green, softly. "She's so upset; she can't even see the wrongs that she's doing. Her mother was exactly the same way. I don't know if that's a good thing or not."

There's no answer. Miss Green turns the computer back off and gets up. She steps back into the store and starts working once again.

Elsewhere, Katie has just shown back up at home. She shrugs off her boots and her rain slick, pulls the bottle of shampoo out of her pocket, and makes a bee line for the bathroom. The bottle of *Wash Away the Blues* shampoo is the same size, shape, and color as her father's usual bottle.

It's easy enough to switch them out. It's easy enough to vanish into her bedroom for the rest of the night, too.

Come morning, she flounces down the stairs, ready for breakfast and another dark day of missing, regretting, and dealing with the seemingly impossible feat of getting through the day.

Her father is at the breakfast table and oodles is wagging his tale waiting for his breakfast. For the first time in a week, her father smiles at Katie, "Hey there! That's my kiddo."

She blinks, startled at the sudden change in demeanor, "Dad?"

"I know this must be hard on you," says Sam. "Why don't we go catch a movie when you get home from school?"

It's Saturday. Katie is so unnerved by the sudden change in attitude that she doesn't correct him.

Over the next week, it just continues to get better – but it also gets worse. Each morning, her father seems a little bit happier, a little bit lighter. But each morning, he seems to be less of himself and more of someone else; someone with more spring in their step, with less recollection of their daily life.

And then, one day, Katie walks down stairs and her father jumps to his feet. He bellows, "Who are you?"

Katie looks around to see who might have just waltzed into her house, but it's empty. "Dad? What's wrong with you?"

"Dad? I don't know what you're talking about, kid, but I'm pretty sure you shouldn't be in my house and take that dog with you," he announces.

"It's *our* house and Oodles stays," stresses Katie, surprised.

"I don't have a clue what you're talking about!" Sam shouts.

"Don't you remember my mother? Isabella?" Katie stammers.

"I've never met an Isabella!" he snorts.

"Never met one?" Katie can't believe her ears. "You were married for almost twenty-four years!"

Sam shakes his head, "You've got the wrong guy. I've never been married."

"You have! You were married and she just died!" Katie says, shocked.

Sam holds his arms out to the side, "Does it look like I'm the sort of guy to have gotten married?"

"You're wearing a ring," stresses Katie, trying hard not to cry. Unshed tears burn her eyes.

Sam looks down at the golden band on his left hand. "That's my class ring. Everyone in my class has one. Listen, kid. I think you've just got the wrong place. You've certainly got the wrong man."

"I don't," insists Katie. "I don't!"

No amount of arguing makes Sam see reason. The pair stand in the middle of the kitchen like strangers; he can't seem to remember her or her mother. Terrified by the strange problem, Katie runs out the front door. She doesn't even put on shoes.

Rain water soaks into her socks. Katie runs until her chest aches and her lungs burn. The young girl races through the pouring rain; races through a city that's turned into gray blocks and gray air; races into Miss Green's shop.

The bell chimes. It mixes with a sob finally wrenching free from Katie; a sob sounding too much like a wounded animal.

Miss Green swoops upon her in a matter of moments, wrapping a worn purple blanket around Katie's shoulder. She says, "You stupid girl! What are you doing running around out here like this? You're going to catch your death!"

"I don't care," sobs Katie. She throws herself around the old woman. Miss Green is little more than flesh stretched over bones, this wisp of a woman that's almost non-existent. "I don't care about that!"

"You will later," assures Miss Green. She ushers Katie inside and sits her down in the office, in that big bear claw chair.

"Now, you sit here and relax. Tell me, did you get into a fight with someone? Is your father doing alright?"

"I'm so sorry," sobs Katie. She hides her face in her palms. Wet hair hangs in her face as she begins to explain, "I stole from you. I don't usually, steal, I mean, but I know you were following me, and I saw that shampoo, and I took it! But now my dad's acting weird!"

Miss Green sighs. She brushes the hair out of Katie's face with her skeletal hand, "Like he doesn't remember you?"

"Exactly!" Katie shouts, stunned that Miss Green already knew it.

"You must get the shampoo back and undo the damage that has been done," Miss Green scolds.

"What damage?" Katie questions. "I thought - I thought it was just soap! Unless... are the rumors true?"

Miss Green gives her a very serious look, "There's a kernel of truth in every rumor. Katie, you have done a horrid thing. You have given your father a cursed object, and now, you must break that curse."

"What?" Katie is shocked.

"Everything in this room is cursed, Miss Green explains. "I break those dark spells before selling them. That shampoo had not yet been fixed."

"How do I help him?" Katie can't believe her ears.

"Train under me," says Miss Green, seriously. "The only way to undo your father's memory loss is to make the green cheesecake."

"The what?" Katie wrinkles her nose.

"It's an ancient recipe, and one that is not made lightly," Miss Green says. "It must be eaten at midnight on the next full moon, lest the effects of the curse become permanent."

Over the next week, Katie's father continues to decline. The effects are more apparent now. Her father believes himself to be a teenager. Each passing day, he becomes less responsible. Work has to be twisted, so that it's treated as school - an obligation that simply can't be avoided.

The whispers are the worst part of all. They spread across the earth like a wild fire.

Did you hear about the Rite man?

I think he's had a nervous breakdown. There's something not right about how he's acting.

That poor daughter. She's gone through so much. You know, my son goes to school with her - what's the name, Kelly? That's it, Kelly. He says that she's not doing well.

Doing better than her father.
That man's on the edge.
That man is about to break.
I wouldn't be surprised if we were forced to have another funeral soon. The only question is; will it be an open casket or a closed one?

She tries to keep her head up. It's hard, though. Going to see Miss Green for *training* is the only thing that really keeps Katie going. They have their first meeting on Saturday. Once more, Katie ventures into the back room.

This time, she takes a moment to look around. There are portraits on the wall, showing pictures of Miss Green and Isabella Rite. They're standing close together in most of them, sometimes even touching.

Miss Green appears as if from the shadows, "Your mother was a dear friend of mine."

"I know she was over here a lot," says Katie. "You were friends?"

"No," says Miss Green. There's a distinct note of sorrow to her face, one that causes a crease to her brow and twist to her mouth. "She was my best student, but we weren't friends."

"You used to be. Didn't you?" Katie asks "When I was little, she would come home and spend hours talking about you."

"When you were young... yes, that was a very long time ago," Miss Green says sadly. "We were friends, once, but then a recipe went horribly wrong. That day, she vowed to never view me as more than a mentor."

Katie asks, "What happened?"

"That's not a story for today," says Miss Green, her voice suddenly sharp. She spins around, all but gliding over to one of the metal book shelves. From there, she pulls out a recipe book. The leather is old and cracked. The pages are yellow with age and filled with small cursive print.

"Please," says Katie. "Tell me what happened with that accident. Did something bad happen to my mother?"

"No," says Miss Green. "I will not talk about it tonight! There's no reason for it. The past shouldn't be forgotten, but it doesn't need to be brought up constantly. Come, look at the recipe."

Katie has no choice but to do as she's told. That first day, they don't even attempt making the green cheesecake. She is simply sat down in the bear claw chair, and she's forced to read it until she can say it all backwards.

That evening, rather than go home, Katie goes to Denny's.

Denny is thrilled to see her. She demands, "Tell me the recipe!"

Katie reads it off without even having to close her eyes, "Eight cups of sugar. Four blocks of cream cheese. A block of soft goat cheese. Four tablespoons of black pepper. A prick of rose water. Two pricks of rose petals, freshly ground. A wedge of garlic, a square of chocolate, and a dash of hot chili pepper."

"That sounds gross," says Denny. "I mean; why would anyone eat that?"

"I don't know," admits Katie. "I'm kind of hoping that this whole thing is just a bad dream or some sort of twisted joke. A prank that my father's playing on me, you know?"

"I knew she was a witch," Denny says smartly.

"She says she's a curse breaker," Katie sighs. "I think she's just a loon."

"She might be a loon," says Denny. "I'm not arguing that. But the fact that you're still not convinced she's a witch is just beyond me! You've heard the rumors about her, right?"

Katie is silent for a long moment. Finally, she says, "Not every rumor is true."

The next day, Katie goes back to Miss Green's shop. Though it hadn't been there yesterday, there is now a massive stove in the middle of the back room. A wooden table has been set up, too, and it's filled up with mixing bowls, spoons, and pans. The ingredients are all sitting out, too, so there's basically nothing that Katie needs to do.

Miss Green waves at the table, "Do you remember the recipe?"

"I do," says Katie.

"Then start cooking," says Miss Green. "Make sure that you don't miss anything."

Katie dumps eight cups of sugar into the mixing bowl. She creams four blocks of cream cheese and one block of soft goat cheese. Then the four tablespoons of black pepper follow.

Katie pauses. She looks at Miss Green, uncertain, "How much is a prick?"

"The same amount as you would bleed should you prick yourself on a rose thorn," says Miss Green.

Katie adds a prick of rose water from a pale pink vial. She adds two pricks of rose petals, freshly ground. A wedge of crushed garlic goes next.

Katie picks up the square of chocolate, "Does this need to be melted or grated?"

"Just put the whole square in," says Miss Green.

"Just like this?" Katie asks.

"Just like that," Miss Green answers.

Katie drops the square of chocolate into the mixing bowl. Then she adds a dash of hot chili pepper.

Finally, the mixture gets dumped into a pan and put into the oven. When it comes out twenty minutes later, firm as a rock, it's a vibrant blue.

"I thought it was supposed to be green?" Katie prods the cheese cake with her batter covered spoon.

Miss Green shakes her head, "It should be. You've simply put too much sorrow into this recipe. Try again, little one."

And so she does.

Katie dumps eight cups of sugar into the mixing bowl. She creams four blocks of cream cheese, and a block of soft goat cheese. Four tablespoons of black pepper follow. She adds a prick of rose water from a pale pink vial. She adds two pricks of rose petals, freshly ground. A wedge of crushed garlic goes next. Then she drops the square of chocolate into the mixing bowl. Then she adds a dash of hot chili pepper.

Trying hard not to sniffle, Katie puts the whit batter into oven. When it comes out twenty minutes later, it's purple. She moans, "What's wrong with it?"

"Your emotions are too wild," says Miss Green. "You must learn to focus them better. You must learn to keep them in check. The blue is the sorrow that seeped into the batter, and the purple claims that you are already despairing. There's no way that it will come out correctly if you're too focused on your own feelings. Try again."

With a forlorn sigh, Katie dumps eight cups of sugar into the mixing bowl. She creams four blocks of cream cheese, and a block of soft goat cheese. Four tablespoons of black pepper follow. She adds a prick of rose water from a pale pink vial. She adds two pricks of rose petals, freshly ground. A wedge of crushed garlic goes next. Then she drops the square of chocolate into the mixing bowl. Then she adds a dash of hot chili pepper.

For the third time, it gets put into the oven. For the third time, it comes out. The cheesecake is green. Overjoyed, Katie sets it down on the table.

"I did it," she says.

"You did," says Miss Green, surprised.

Suddenly, the cake turns the colors of the rainbow. Mrs. Green bursts into laughter. "That's new," she says. "I don't think I've ever seen that happen before. I will have to look that up and get back to you on what it means."

Mrs. Green says between laughs, "That's enough for today though, Katie. Good job!"

It's been a long day, but it hasn't been a bad one. Katie enjoys mixing the ingredients for the cheesecake and can't help but feel hopeful.

By the time she gets home, the hope has vanished. There's a strange car in her driveway. When Katie steps into the living room, she sees him curled up on the couch with a younger woman, all bleach blonde hair and ruby painted lips.

Sam looks up at her, "Hey there, roomie. What's the look for?"

"Who's that?" Katie folds her arms over her chest.

"My new girlfriend," says Sam, throwing an arm over the blonde. "This is Rosa."

Rosa waves at Katie.

Katie gapes, "Your girlfriend?"

"That's what I said," Sam taps Rosa on the shoulder. "She's a little weird, but she keeps the place clean and she's not that loud. Good enough for a roommate."

"You bastard," spits Katie. The curse falls from her tongue like molten silver. Rage dances through her veins. She points at her father with a trembling hand, "How could you do this to her? How could you do this to me?"

"What are you talking about?" Sam says, shocked at Katie's outburst.

"It's not even been a full month! It's been - it's been a handful of days!" Katie shouts, "Why would you do this? Why would you do this to me?"

Sam looks bewildered, "I don't have a clue what you're talking about, Katie Cat."

"Don't call me that," spits Katie. "Don't you dare call me that!"

Rosa stands up, "I should leave."

"No," says Sam.

At the same time, Katie snarls, "Get out of my house."

Rosa hurries outside. Katie is hot on her heels. The two teenagers go separate ways, rushing down the sidewalks for places unknown. The night stretches on. Eventually, Katie has no choice but to go back home. It's cold out, and she doesn't have a jacket.

The house is dark. Katie turns on the light in the living room. She goes to the corner shelf and pulls out the family photo album. Then she goes into the kitchen and starts to cook.

All night, Katie slaves over the stove. She thinks about the cheesecake, the cursed shampoo, and the loss of everything. Come morning, she has made a great spread of breakfast foods.

Sam asks, "Is this to make up for your break down?"

"Can I show you something?" Katie asks softly.

"Question with a question. That's cool," Sam sits down.

Katie sits down next to him. She sets down the photo album and flips to one of the early pages. It's filled with wedding pictures. "This is you."

Sam frowns, "Yeah, that does look like me."

Katie taps the picture of her mom, "This is Isabella Rite. She was your wife for over twenty years. She was my mom, too."

"I don't recognize her. I don't remember being there, either," Sam says, surprised.

"What about these?" Katie flips the page. She brings up pictures of her mother, pregnant; her parents at Christmas; the day that she was born.

Still, there's nothing. There's not even a hint of recognition on Sam's face, "I'm sorry. I know that looks like me, but I don't remember any of that."

Katie's heart sinks, "What *do* you remember?"

Sam is silent for a long moment. Finally, he says, "I remember getting my first car the day that I turned eighteen. It was red. I really loved that car. Do you know what happened to it?"

"It's gone," says Katie, softly. "You crashed it on the second date with my mother. Rather than fix it, you paid to have her arm set."

"Oh," says Sam. "I don't remember that. Should I tell you that I'm sorry?"

"Are you?" she asks.

"No," Sam shrugs.

"Then you shouldn't say it," Katie says walking away.

School is horrible the next day. Everything reminds her of the loss that she's suffered; the kids talk just as much as the adults, maybe even a little bit more.

Do you think that she's going to lose it too?

I think she already has. That girl's been spending all kinds of time with the old loon. You know, the one on the square?

Did you see how she came in today? Look at her hair!

Her hair? Forget that. Look at her face!

There's a lot of laughter, too. Everyone stares at Katie. She feels like an ant in a glass tank, like someone that's been put up on display. By lunch time, even Denny is giving her odd looks.

Denny asks, "Are you okay?"

"I'm fine," snaps Katie.

"You don't look fine," Deny argues.

"Well, I am!" Katie snaps again.

Denny shakes her head, "Whatever you say, Katie Cat."

Katie Cat.

The words dig into Katie's heart like rusty nails. She jumps to her feet, shaking her head, "I can't do this anymore! I can't *be* here! This place is too much, Denny! Do you hear what everyone's saying?"

Brazenly, Tabby asks, "Is it true?"

Denny elbows Tabby in the side, "Why would you ask that?"

"Because I wanted to know," snaps Tabby. "You wanted to know, too! You're the one that brought it up earlier!"

Denny's eyes go wide. She spins around to look at Katie, but the other girl has already taken off, racing out of the cafeteria, out of the school, out of every place that once felt like home.

It's still raining.

It feels like it's always going to be raining.

Without knowing where else to go, Katie heads to Miss Green's shop. She lets herself in. The bell chimes.

"Katie? You're here early," says Miss Green. "Is everything okay?"

Katie ignores her. She dashes into the back room, grabbing a bottle of *Forgetful Tonic* off one of the nearby shelves. "Make things better," begs Katie, and then she pulls off the cork topper and downs the liquid.

It tastes like copper, and ocean water, and a blazingly hot summer day. Katie has half the bottle gone before Miss Green steps into the room. She shakes her head; the sorrow is etched into her face, in those too large eyes, in those chapped and twisted lips. "I'm sorry, Katie. That isn't going to make you forget. That tonic, it's meant to help you remember things. Haven't you ever read the label?"

The bottle falls from Katie's hand. Pale pink sugar water spills out over the floor. She sobs. It makes her throat burn. Hot tears spill down her cheeks, "I don't want to do this anymore, Miss Green! I can't go back to that house! I just - I can't!"

Miss Green picks up the bottle. She runs her thumb over the label.

Forgetful Tonic

For those who can't remember what they've forgotten

For those who can't avoid important dates

Drink the full bottle on a sunny day in July

right after it rains

when the clouds are soft and white

The old woman shakes her head, "Katie, this won't do anything for you. You know everything that you need too. This won't help you remember the past, because you haven't forgotten it."

"Can't I give it to my father?" Katie sobs.

"It won't help, because he doesn't want to remember," Miss Green says.

"*I* want him to remember," wails Katie.

Miss Green says, "That's not enough. Only the green cheesecake can make him remember. I've told you this."

"I can't make it turn green! The rainbow wasn't enough, was it?" Katie cries.

"No, dear. The rainbow wasn't enough," Miss Green says taking Katie's hand. "The rainbow simply showed that you were confused. I understand, Katie. You've been through so much these last few weeks. I can't imagine going through this at your age. But do you know something? The rainbow was also a sign of hope."

Katie sniffs. She scrubs her face with the back of her hand, "I don't feel very hopeful."

"Do you think that your father might one day return to his normal self?" Miss Green sets the pink glass bottle down on the counter. She pulls a chocolate bar off of one of the shelves. The wrapper is made of gold foil, with small white print on it. The print is all over the foil, but it just reads *chocolate* in countless different languages.

"I don't know," admits Katie.

Miss Green says, "That's why it came out rainbow. But you're getting close. If you turn that hope into faith, then you might be able to make the cheesecake turn green. You have the time, Katie."

"I don't want to spend any more time like this," says Katie, near frantic. "My father doesn't remember anything. He brought home a girl from my school and tried to date her!"

"He doesn't know better. Not now, at least. But soon," says Miss Green. "Soon, Katie."

Katie shakes her head. She doesn't know what else to say, because there are no words to express her grief, sorrow, or rage.

"Then eat this," says Miss Green. "You're a good girl, Katie. This will give you the courage to face what you cannot undo and to correct what you can."

Katie grabs the chocolate and eats it. It's sweet, sickly sweet. The chocolate clings to her tongue. It soaks into her taste buds, into her very pores - and just like that, she knows.

Memories, even the painful ones, serve a purpose. Life is worth living. It's worth remembering. Katie hums in delight. She says, "Thank you, Miss Green. Do you think - could we try making the cheesecake again?"

"Of course," says Miss Green. She sets up the table, "Here, Katie. Remember what that chocolate made you feel. Believe in yourself and the people around you."

"I will," promises Katie, and then she dumps eight cups of sugar into the mixing bowl. She creams four blocks of cream cheese and a block of soft goat cheese. Four tablespoons of black pepper follow. She adds a prick of rose water from a pale pink vial. She adds two pricks of rose petals, freshly ground. A wedge of crushed garlic goes next. Then she drops the square of chocolate into the mixing bowl. Then she adds a dash of hot chili pepper.

The cheesecake goes into the oven. When Katie takes it out twenty minutes later, it's green. She sets it down on the table and holds her breath.

It stays green.

One minute passes. Two-minutes pass by. Three, four, five-minutes pass by, and the cheesecake stays green.

"I did it," breathes Katie. She glances up, looking at Miss Green. "Did I do it?"

"You did," says Miss Green, and she sounds ridiculously surprised. "Katie, you did it. So long as you can get your father to eat this on midnight of the full moon, then things will go back to normal."

Katie can't control her tears. She cries in relief. Then, she throws herself at Miss Green and hugs the older woman. "Thank you! Thank you so much! Tell me what I can do to pay you back for this, please! Anything!"

"There is one thing," admits Miss Green. "If you can get your father to eat this, things will go back to normal. Remember that. Realize that. When things are normal and you truly believe in the power of that cheesecake, come back here."

"Why?" Katie asks.

"Because I am an old woman, and this is a dark world." Miss Green replies. "There are many curses that have been placed on this land. I can't take care of them all on my own, not anymore."

Surprised, Katie pulls away and asks, "You want me to help you break curses?"

"Not just any curse," says Miss Green. "I need help breaking the curses of the Greek Gods!"

"Those aren't real," says Katie, but even she can't believe her protest. She just made a green cheesecake, after all, and ate mind restoring chocolate.

"They are," says Miss Green. "And, more than just a favor, I'll turn it into a deal. You asked me why your mother never came back."

Katie perks up, "You'll tell me?"

"More than that," says Miss Green. "I'll help you fix the problem that she created."

Later that month, on the night of the full moon, Katie sets the green cheesecake out on the table. She cuts a piece for herself and one for Sam. Then she calls him downstairs.

"What's going on?" Sam yawns, and scrubs at his face like a child.

Katie gives him the warmest smile she can muster, "Just a tradition of mine. I make it every year on this night. I thought that, since we got off on such a rocky start, it might be nice to include you."

Sam looks surprised. Still, he sits down and picks up a fork, "I'm never one to turn down sweets."

"No," says Katie, smiling. "You really aren't."

The grandfather clock in the hallway chimes midnight. Sam takes a bite of the cheesecake. A look of utter bliss crosses his face.

Katie watches with bated breath. When he swallows it, she asks, "What do you think?"

Sam smiles at her, "I think you've been practicing! This is great, Katie!"

She can't tell if it's Sam the teenager or Sam her father, "Really?"

"Yeah, Katie Cat. You've done great. Your mother would have been proud of this. The color's a little strange, but the taste is right on mark."

"What?" Katie stares at him.

"I know," says Sam. "Your life's probably been real topsy-turvy lately. That's why we're eating at midnight, huh?"

Katie is struck speechless. She nods.

Sam says, "Well, honey, things will get better. I know it seems dark right now but - "

"Dad," squeals, Katie, flinging herself at Sam. "I'm so glad to hear that. I'm so, so glad to hear that."

The next day, Katie shows up at Miss Green's shop. She smiles at the old woman, "Okay, Miss Green. I'll work on these curses for you."

Miss Green smiles at Katie, "Your father is feeling better, then?"

"Much better," Katie smiles.

"Good. Then we shall start right away!" Miss Green announces. "The cheesecake, it can break almost any curse, so long as you're able to alter it enough."

"Alter it?" Katie questions. "But I've only just mastered making it green!"

Miss Green laughs, "You haven't mastered anything, darling. You will, though." She wraps an arm around Katie's waist. "Come with me. Let me tell you the tale of Medusa."

THE APOTHECARY

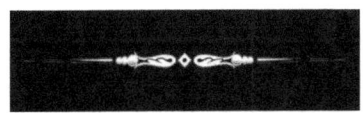

Green Cheesecake at Midnight

Please read our other series

1. The Lunar Princess
2. Mr. Inventions
3. Alley Pop Girls
4. Twinkle Twinkle Little Star
5. Faye and Spot

T.S. Cherry

www.ingramcontent.com/pod-product-compliance
Lightning Source LLC
Chambersburg PA
CBHW071542080526
44588CB00011B/1755